CHARACTER EDUCATION

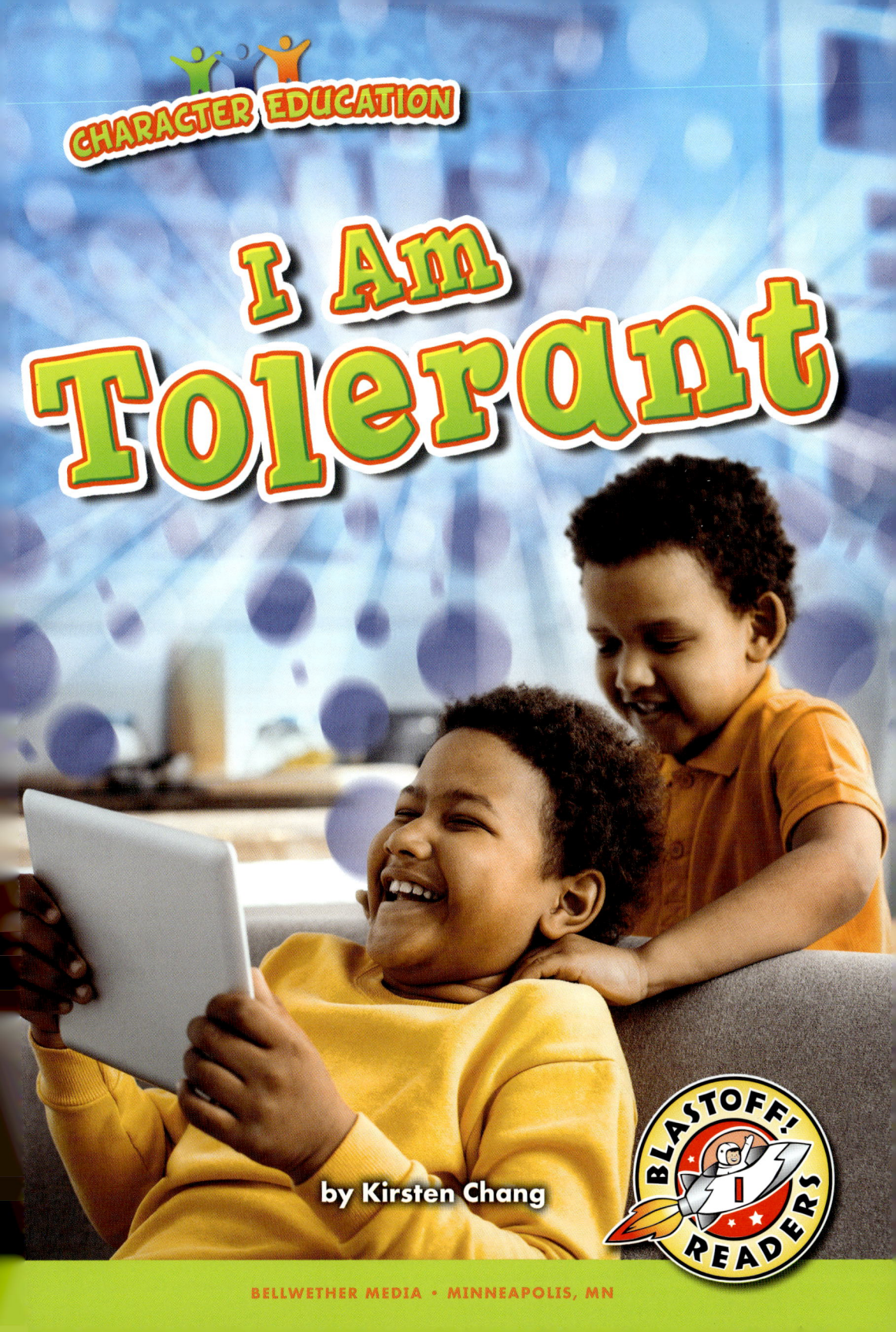

I Am Tolerant

by Kirsten Chang

BLASTOFF! READERS

BELLWETHER MEDIA • MINNEAPOLIS, MN

Note to Librarians, Teachers, and Parents:

Blastoff! Readers are carefully developed by literacy experts and combine standards-based content with developmentally appropriate text.

Level 1 provides the most support through repetition of high-frequency words, light text, predictable sentence patterns, and strong visual support.

Level 2 offers early readers a bit more challenge through varied simple sentences, increased text load, and less repetition of high-frequency words.

Level 3 advances early-fluent readers toward fluency through increased text and concept load, less reliance on visuals, longer sentences, and more literary language.

Level 4 builds reading stamina by providing more text per page, increased use of punctuation, greater variation in sentence patterns, and increasingly challenging vocabulary.

Level 5 encourages children to move from "learning to read" to "reading to learn" by providing even more text, varied writing styles, and less familiar topics.

Whichever book is right for your reader, Blastoff! Readers are the perfect books to build confidence and encourage a love of reading that will last a lifetime!

This edition first published in 2020 by Bellwether Media, Inc.

No part of this publication may be reproduced in whole or in part without written permission of the publisher. For information regarding permission, write to Bellwether Media, Inc., Attention: Permissions Department, 6012 Blue Circle Drive, Minnetonka, MN 55343.

Library of Congress Cataloging-in-Publication Data

Names: Chang, Kirsten, 1991- author.
Title: I Am Tolerant / by Kirsten Chang.
Description: Minneapolis : Bellwether Media, 2020. | Series: Character education | Includes bibliographical references and index. | Audience: Ages 5-8 | Audience: Grades K-1 | Summary: ""Developed by literacy experts for students in kindergarten through grade three, this book introduces tolerance to young readers through leveled text and related photos"--Provided by publisher"
Identifiers: LCCN 2019024636 (print) | LCCN 2019024637 (ebook) | ISBN 9781644871140 (library binding) | ISBN 9781618917942 (paperback) | ISBN 9781618917843 (ebook)
Subjects: LCSH: Toleration--Juvenile literature.
Classification: LCC HM1271 .C475 2020 (print) | LCC HM1271 (ebook) | DDC 179/.9--dc23
LC record available at https://lccn.loc.gov/2019024636
LC ebook record available at https://lccn.loc.gov/2019024637

Text copyright © 2020 by Bellwether Media, Inc. BLASTOFF! READERS and associated logos are trademarks and/or registered trademarks of Bellwether Media, Inc.

Editor: Christina Leaf   Designer: Jeffrey Kollock

Printed in the United States of America, North Mankato, MN.

Table of Contents

What Is Tolerance?	4
Why Be Tolerant?	10
You Are Tolerant!	16
Glossary	22
To Learn More	23
Index	24

What Is Tolerance?

Laila is new in school. She is from another country.

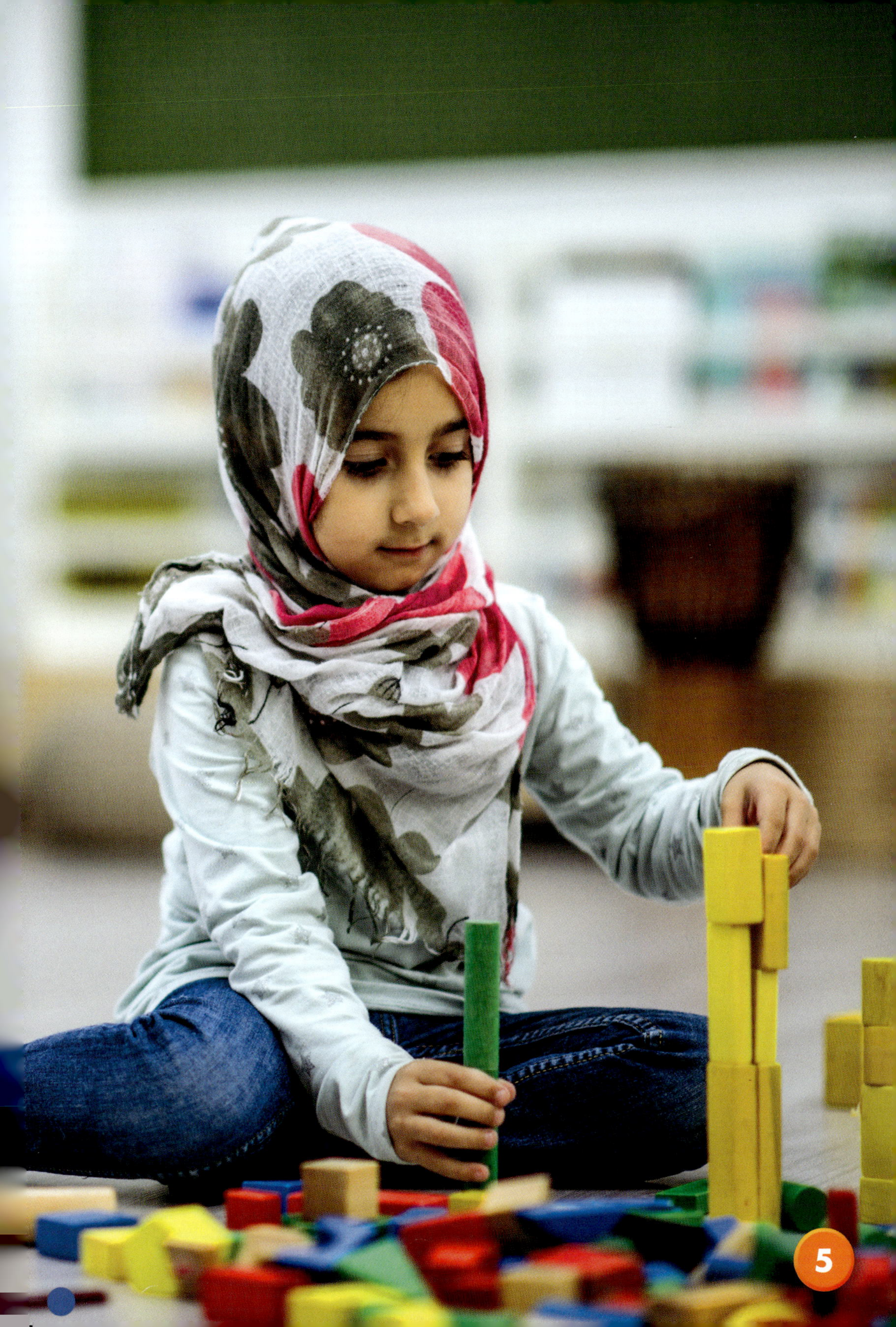

Do you call her
a mean name?
Or are you tolerant?

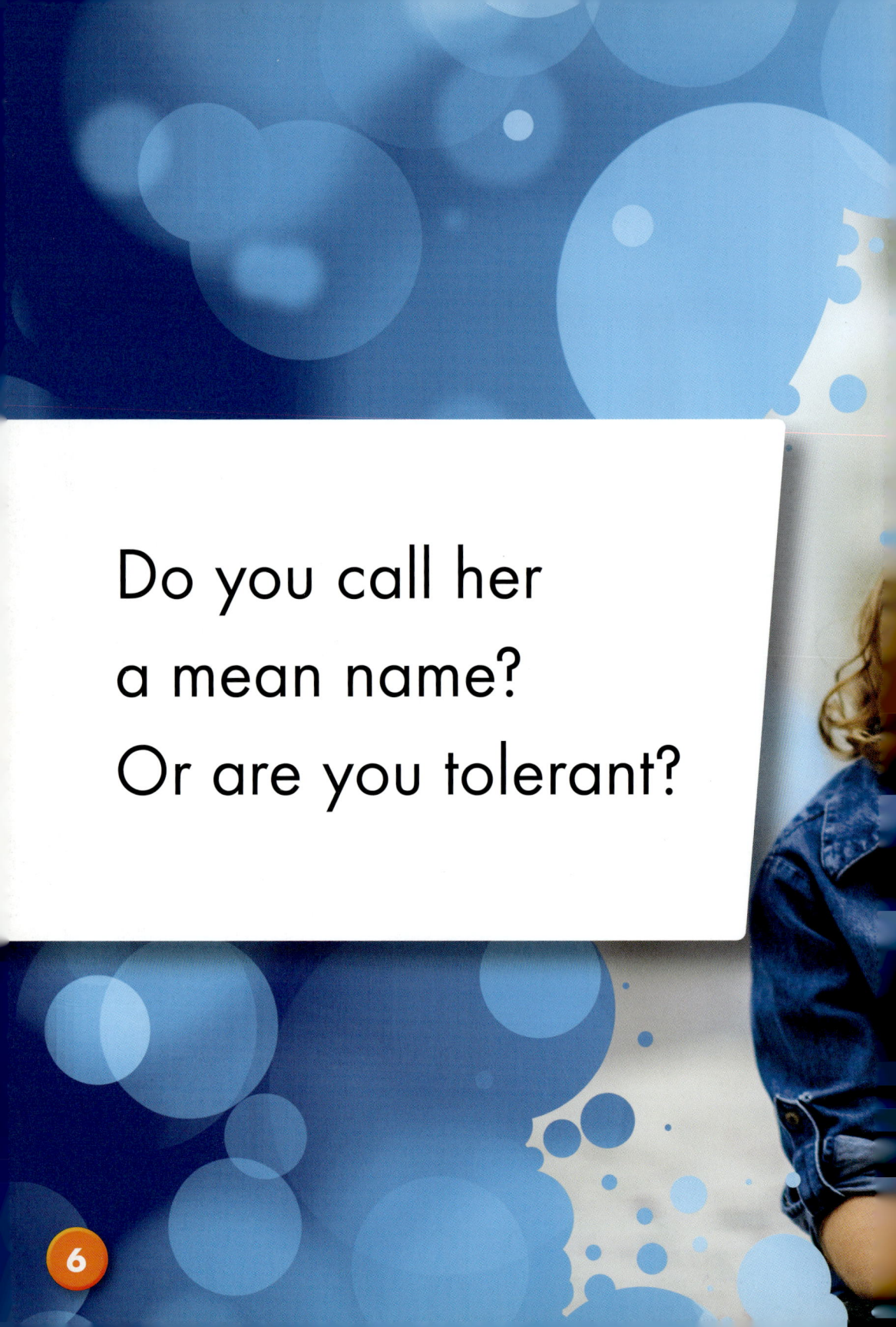

7

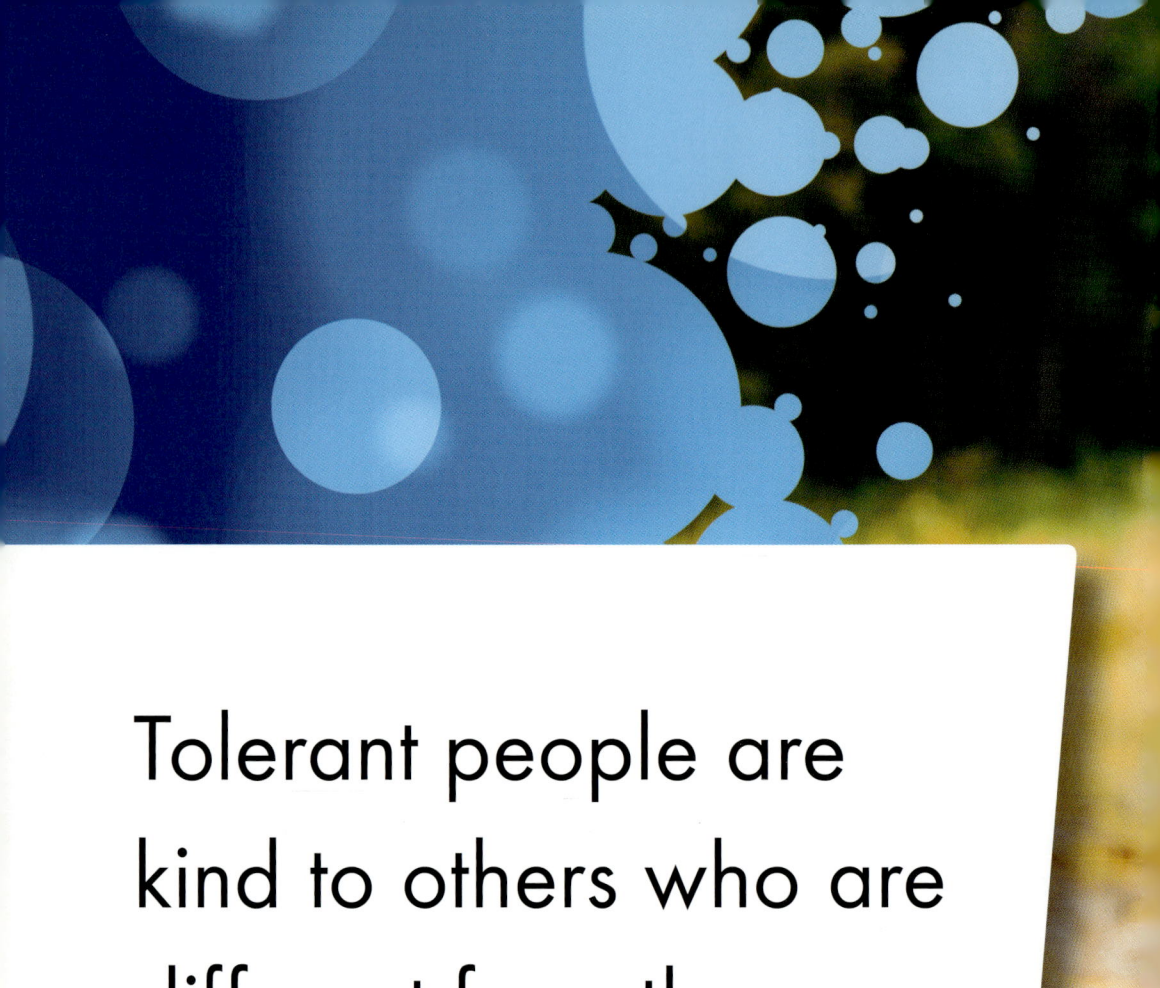

Tolerant people are kind to others who are different from them.

9

Why Be Tolerant?

We are all different! Our differences make us special.

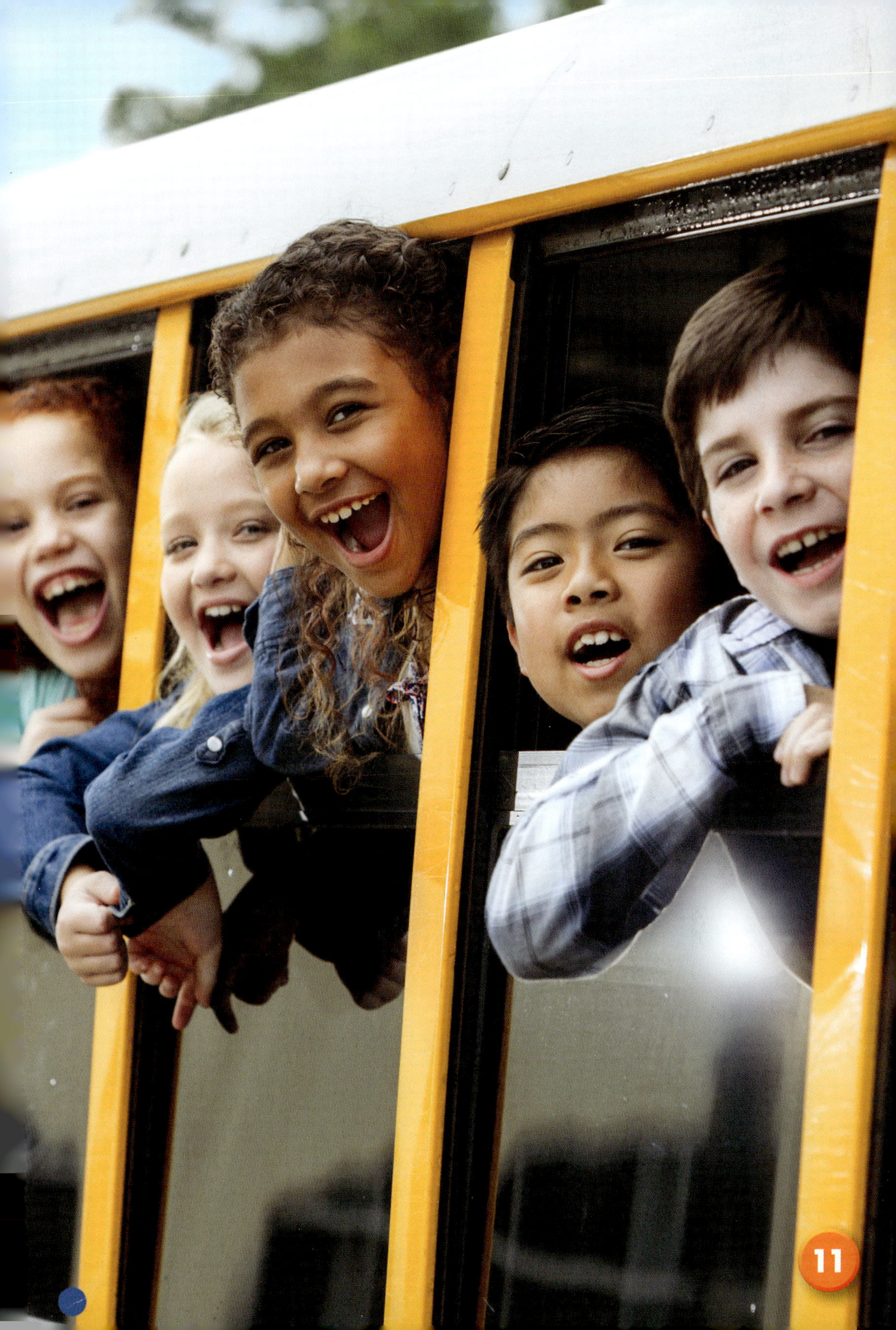

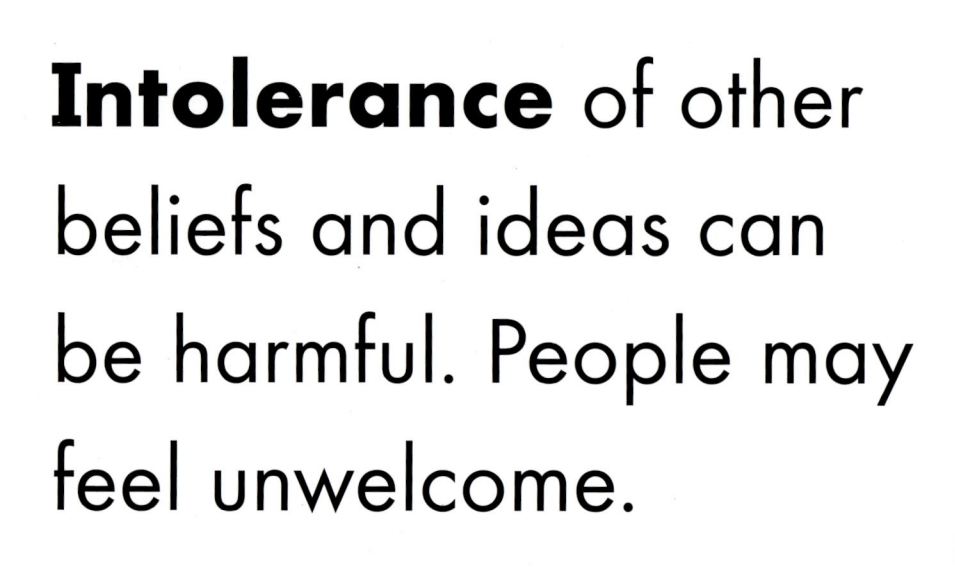

Intolerance of other beliefs and ideas can be harmful. People may feel unwelcome.

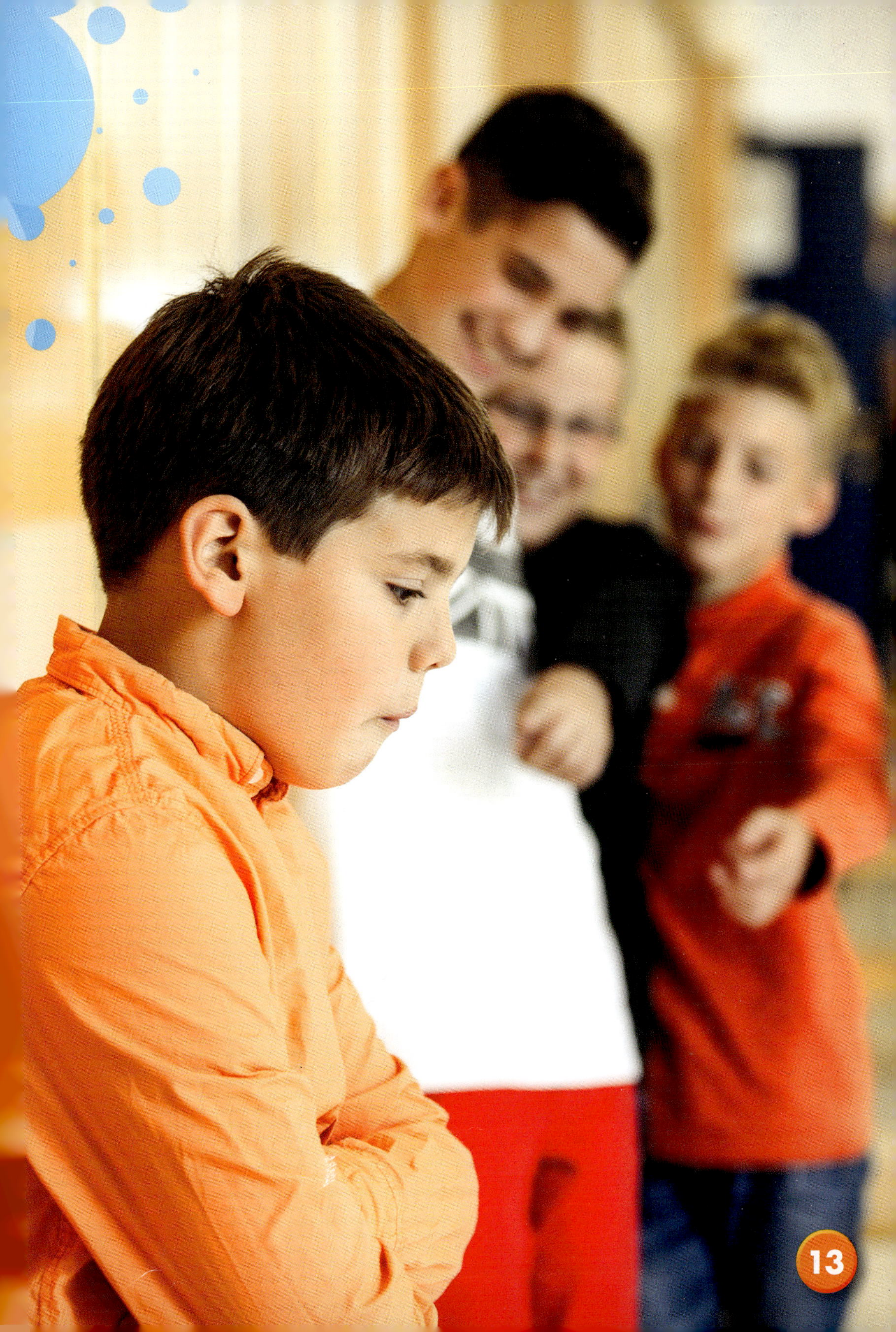

Tolerance makes the world safer and more **peaceful**!

Who Is Tolerant?

15

You Are Tolerant!

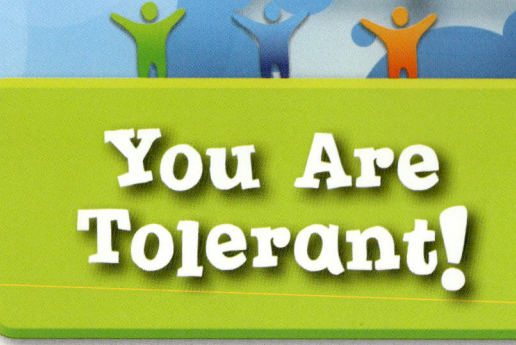

You can be tolerant! Eric never makes fun of anyone.

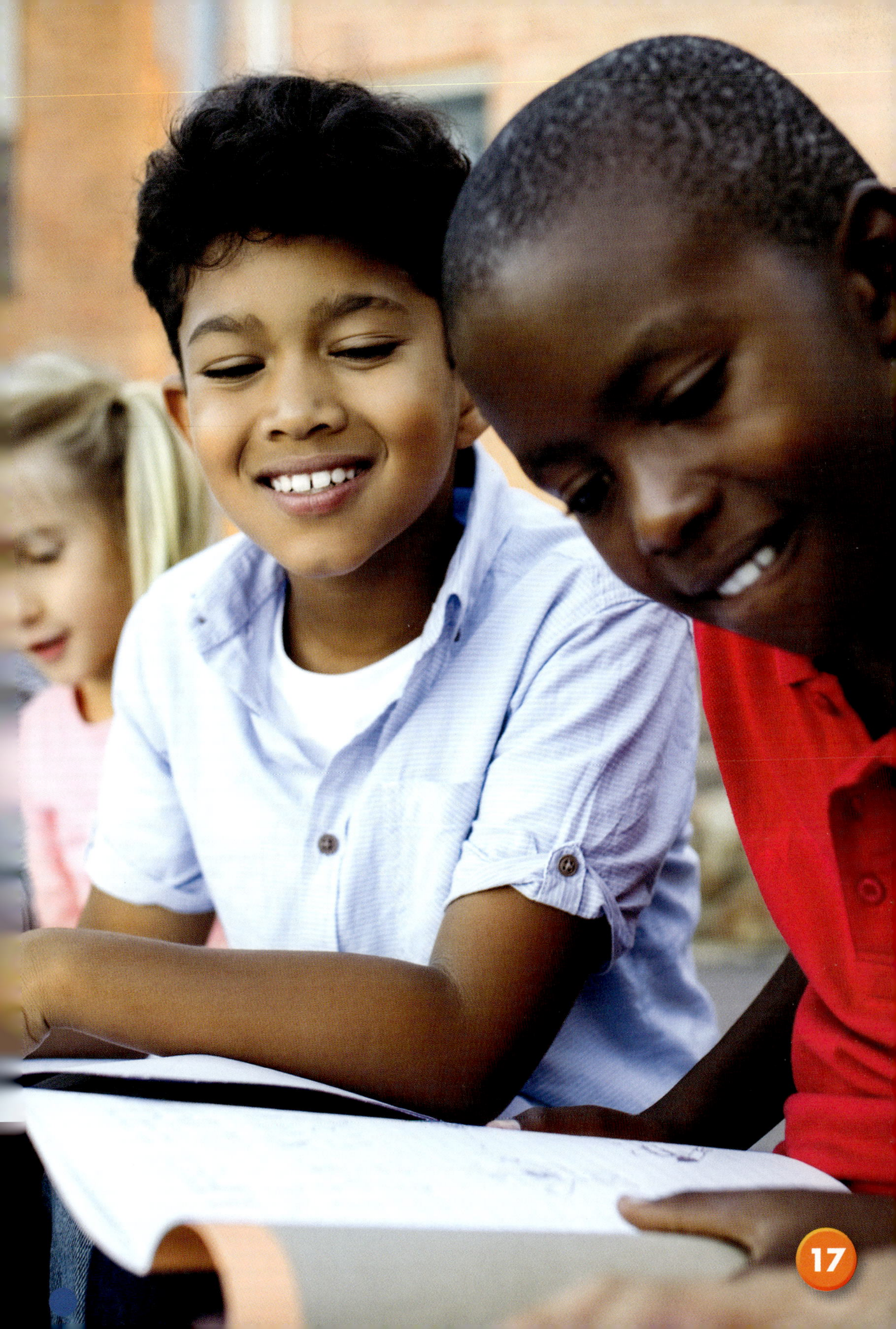

Ann and Dev **disagree**. Dev listens carefully to Ann's **opinions**.

19

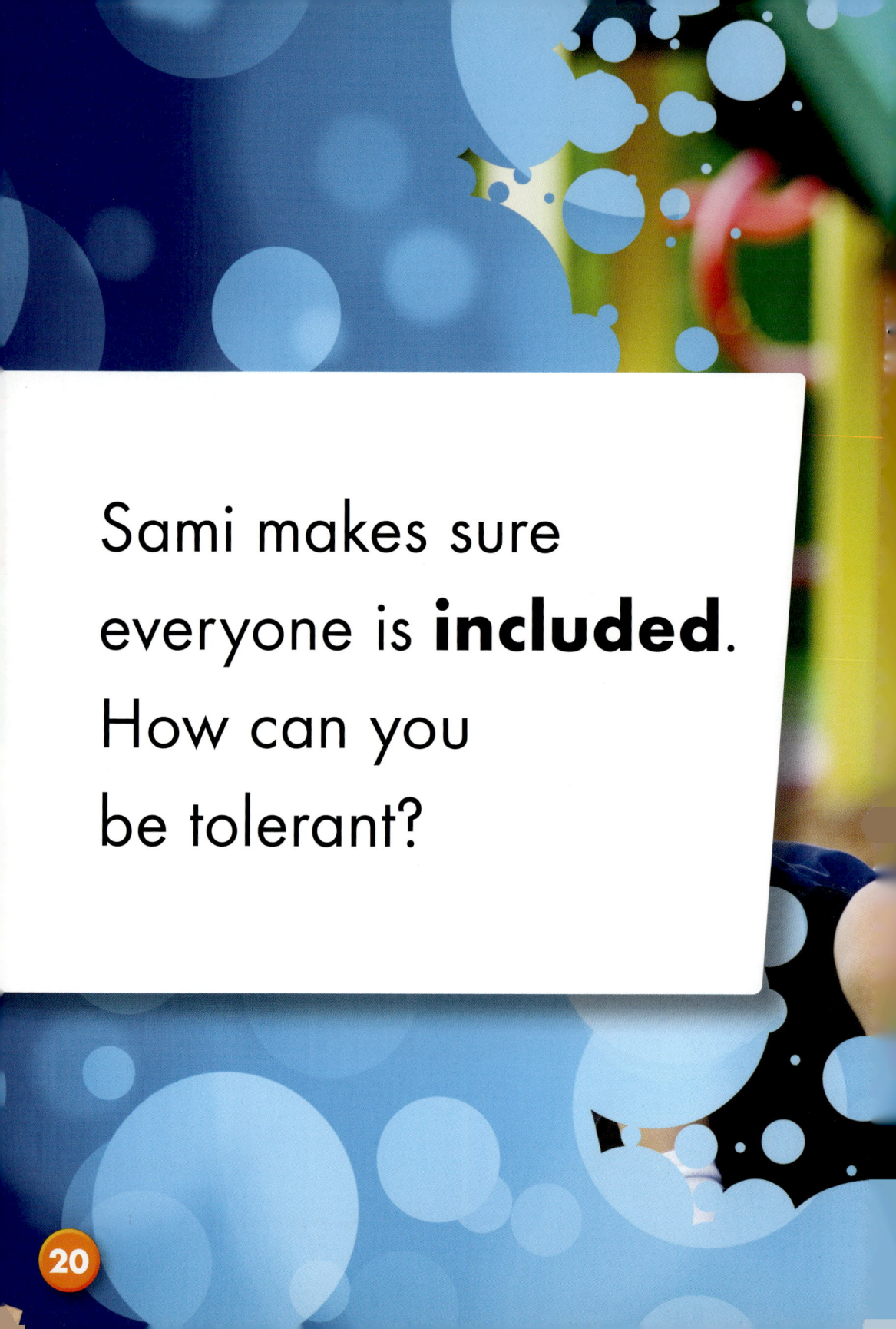

Sami makes sure everyone is **included**. How can you be tolerant?

21

Glossary

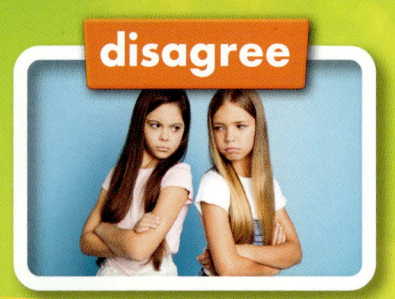

disagree

to have different thoughts or ideas

opinions

views or ideas about a particular subject

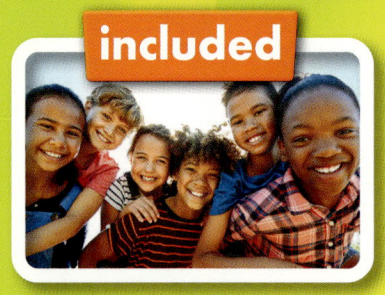

included

to be part of a larger group

peaceful

related to a pleasant situation without fighting

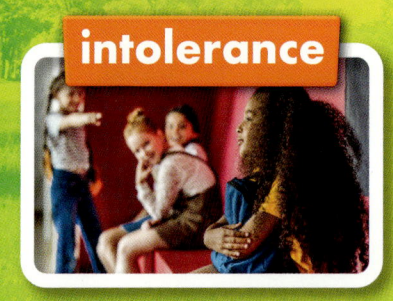

intolerance

the act of not accepting differences

To Learn More

AT THE LIBRARY
Cavell-Clarke, Steffi. *Celebrating Different Beliefs*. New York, N.Y.: Crabtree Publishing Company, 2017.

Fretland VanVoorst, Jenny. *I Am Respectful*. Minneapolis, Minn.: Bellwether Media, 2019.

James, Emily. *How To Be Tolerant: A Question and Answer Book About Tolerance*. North Mankato, Minn.: Capstone Press, 2017.

ON THE WEB

FACTSURFER

Factsurfer.com gives you a safe, fun way to find more information.

1. Go to www.factsurfer.com.

2. Enter "tolerant" into the search box and click 🔍.

3. Select your book cover to see a list of related web sites.

Index

beliefs, 12
country, 4
different, 8, 10
disagree, 18
feel, 12
ideas, 12
included, 20
intolerance, 12
kind, 8
listens, 18
makes fun, 16
name, 6
opinions, 18
school, 4
special, 10

Who Is?, 15
world, 14

The images in this book are reproduced through the courtesy of: Dmytro Zinkevych, front cover; Fat Camera, pp. 4-5, 6-7; Svitlana Bezuhlova, pp. 8-9; kali9, pp. 10-11; funstock, pp. 12-13; Monkey Business Images, pp. 14-15, 22 (included); Oksana Shufrych, p. 15 (bottom left, bottom right); Rido, pp. 16-17; InesBazdar, pp. 18-19; Jaren Jai Wicklund, pp. 20-21; Roman Samborskyi, p. 22 (disagree); LightField Studios, p. 22 (intolerance); imtmphoto, p. 22 (opinions); Rawpixel.com, p. 22 (peaceful).

Children's 179.9 CHA
Chang, Kirsten, 1991-
I am tolerant

06/03/20